Idlis & Dosas

TARLA DALAL
India's # 1 Cookery Author

S&C

SANJAY & CO.
MUMBAI

Ninth Printing : 2008

ISBN : 978-8-186469-48-4

Price: Rs. 89/-

Published & Distributed by : **Sanjay & Company**
353/A-1, Shah & Nahar Industrial Estate, Dhanraj Mill Compound, Lower Parel (W), Mumbai - 400 013. INDIA.
Tel. : (91-22) 2496 8068 • Fax : (91-22) 2496 5876 • E-mail : sanjay@tarladalal.com

UK and USA customers can call us on :
UK : 02080029533 ● USA : 213-634-1406
For books, Membership on **tarladalal.com**, Subscription for **Cooking & More** and Recipe queries
Timing : 9.30 a.m. to 7.00 p.m. (IST), from Monday to Saturday
Local call charges applicable

| Recipe Research & Production Design Arati Fedane | Copy Editor Nisha Katira | Photography Jignesh Jhaveri | Designed by Satyamangal Rege |
| | Food Styling Shubhangi Dhaimade | Typesetting Adityas Enterprises | Printed by : Minal Sales Agencies, Mumbai |

BULK PURCHASES : Tarla Dalal Cookbooks are ideal gifts. If you are interested in buying more than 500 assorted copies of Tarla Dalal Cookbooks at special prices, please contact us at 91-22-2496 8068 or email : sanjay@tarladalal.com

◎ **INTRODUCTION** ◎

Idlis and Dosas are essentially South Indian snacks. However, due to their popularity, they are now available almost everywhere in India. The humble dosa has put South India on every culinary hot spot of the world.

This book is a small but delightful collection of recipes which are a gateway to a whole new world of idlis and dosas. The Corn Idli, Soya Dosa and Tricolour Uttapam will surely amaze you. I have also included recipes of mouth-watering Appam and Appes as well as some accompaniments without which South Indian snacks are incomplete. My personal favourite is the Corn Sambhar which is made without any dal. Surprise your family and friends with the inspiring variety of dishes like the South Indian Sizzler and Dosa Lasagne made using left-over idlis and dosas.

Every recipe is double tested and quantified by me and my research team so as to enable you to get the best results every time.

This book is dedicated to all my readers whose love for new recipes continues to inspire me to create them.

5

⏵ **CONTENTS** ⏴

IDLIS

○ Steam the idlis in an idli steamer with an idli stand or in a pressure cooker. The time taken is less for steaming in a pressure cooker.

○ Always wash, dry and grease the idli moulds.

○ You can use a small piece of wet muslin cloth or a soft banana leaf to cover the mould so that the idlis unmould easily.

○ Always fill the batter into three-quarter of the mould so that there is sufficient space for rising after they are steamed.

○ Allow the steamed idlis to cool slightly before unmoulding them.

○ The idli batter should not be thick but light. Mix the batter using a ladle starting from the bottom of the vessel as rice flour being heavier than urad dal paste, tends to settle down at the base.

○ The secret of making good idlis lies in the urad dal paste. The softer and creamier the paste, the lighter will be the idlis.

๑ IDLI ๏

Picture on cover.

The traditional idli recipe from South Indian kitchens.

Preparation time: 15 minutes.   Cooking time: 45 minutes.   Makes 30 idlis.
Soaking time: 2 to 3 hours.   Fermenting time: Overnight.

3 cups parboiled rice
1 cup split black gram (urad dal)
salt to taste
oil for greasing

1. Wash and soak the rice and urad dal in lukewarm water for 2 to 3 hours.
2. Drain, wash and grind to a smooth paste.
3. Cover and keep aside overnight to ferment.
4. Put spoonfuls of the batter into greased idli moulds and steam for 15 minutes.
   Serve hot with coconut chutney, page 73, or sambhar, page 84.

⊙ POHA IDLI ⊙

A *white and spongy idli.*

Preparation time: 20 minutes.   Cooking time: 10 minutes.   Makes 12 to 15 idlis.
Soaking time: 2 hours.   Fermenting time: 6 to 8 hours.

1 cup rice semolina (idli rawa)
¼ cup beaten rice (jada poha)
¼ cup split black gram (urad dal)
salt to taste
oil for greasing

1. Wash and soak the idli rawa and beaten rice in water for at least 2 hours.
2. Wash the urad dal thoroughly and soak it in water for at least 2 hours.
3. Blend the idli rawa and beaten rice in a blender to make a smooth batter.
4. Then grind the urad dal separately to a smooth paste using a little water.
5. Mix the two batters and add salt. Cover and keep aside for 6 to 8 hours for fermenting.
6. Spoon out the batter into greased idli moulds and steam for 7 to 10 minutes.
   Serve hot with sambhar, page 84.

ଚ **KANCHIPURAM IDLI** ଚ

Mildly *spiced traditional idlis.*

Preparation time: 10 minutes.   Cooking time: 20 minutes.   Makes 15 idlis.
Soaking time: 4 hours.   Fermenting time: 6 to 8 hours.

1 cup split black gram (urad dal)
1 cup raw rice
1 tbsp split Bengal gram (chana dal)
¾ cup sour curds
8 cashewnuts
4 green chillies, chopped
½ coconut, grated
1 tsp grated ginger
½ tsp pepper powder
3 to 4 curry leaves (kadi patta)
2 tbsp ghee
salt to taste

oil for greasing

1. Wash and soak the urad dal and rice together for at least 4 hours.
2. Soak the chana dal separately.
3. Grind the urad dal and rice to a coarse paste using enough water.
4. Allow it to ferment in a warm place for at least 6 to 8 hours.
5. Add the curds, cashewnuts, green chillies, coconut, ginger, pepper powder, curry leaves, ghee, salt and the soaked chana dal and mix well.
6. Spoon the batter into greased idli moulds and steam for 10 to 12 minutes.
7. Repeat with the remaining batter to make more idlis.
   Serve hot with chutney.

༄ SAVOURY IDLI ༄

A *new way of presenting traditional idlis on a banana leaf.*

Preparation time: 30 minutes.   Cooking time: 10 minutes.   Makes 12 to 15 idlis.
Soaking time: 2 hours.   Fermenting time: 6 to 8 hours.

banana leaves, cut into rounds
1 recipe poha idli batter, page 10
1 recipe potato bhaji, page 82
¼ cup curry leaves chutney powder, page 81
oil for greasing

1. Grease the banana leaf rounds and place in an idli stand.
2. Sprinkle some chutney powder on each banana leaf round.
3. Top with some potato bhaji and then 2 tbsp of the idli batter.
4. Steam for 10 to 12 minutes.
5. Cool slightly and unmould the idlis.
    Serve hot.

✑ VERMICELLI NUT IDLI ✑

Unusual idlis made with vermicelli and semolina. Quick to make and mildly spiced.

Preparation time: 15 minutes.   Cooking time: 10 minutes.   Makes 12 idlis.
Soaking time: No soaking.   Fermenting time: 30 minutes.

1 cup broken vermicelli (135 grams)
½ cup semolina (rawa)
1 cup curds
1 tbsp fruit salt
3 tbsp oil
salt to taste
oil for greasing

For the tempering
1 tbsp broken cashewnuts
2 tsp split black gram (urad dal)
½ tsp mustard seeds (rai)
4 chopped green chillies

3 to 4 curry leaves (kadi patta)
a pinch asafoetida (hing)
1 tbsp oil

1. Roast the broken vermicelli in 1½ tbsp of oil till golden brown. Keep aside.
2. In the remaining 1½ tbsp of oil, roast the semolina till light brown. Keep aside.
3. Combine the vermicelli, semolina, curds, salt and 1½ cups of water and keep aside for at least 30 minutes.
4. To prepare the tempering, fry the cashewnuts and the urad dal till golden brown. Add the mustard seeds, green chillies, curry leaves and asafoetida and fry till the mustard seeds crackle. Pour into the idli batter.
5. Add the fruit salt and mix well. Immediately pour into greased idli moulds and steam for 10 minutes.
   Serve hot with a chutney of your choice.

☙ VEGETABLE IDLI ☙

Picture on page 1.

Nutritious vegetable idlis.

Preparation time: 20 minutes.   Cooking time: 20 minutes.   Makes 15 to 20 idlis.

Soaking time: 2 hours.   Fermenting time: 3 to 4 hours.

1 coconut, grated
¼ cup split black gram (urad dal)
2 cups parboiled rice
1 onion, finely chopped
1 carrot, grated
½ cup cabbage, grated
1 tsp cumin seeds (jeera)
4 chopped green chillies
2 tbsp grated coconut
salt to taste
oil for greasing

1. Grind the coconut with 2 cups of warm water and strain to extract the milk. Keep it aside.
2. Wash and soak the urad dal and parboiled rice together for at least 2 hours.
3. Drain and grind to a fine paste using the coconut milk.
4. Add the onion, carrot, cabbage, cumin seeds, green chillies, coconut and salt and mix well. Cover and allow to ferment for 3 to 4 hours.
5. Pour into greased idli moulds and steam for 10 to 12 minutes. Serve hot.

✑ DAL AND VEGETABLE IDLI ✑

These nutritious idlis are slightly heavier than the regular idlis. This batter also makes delicious pancakes.

Preparation time: 15 minutes.   Cooking time: 10 to 12 minutes.   Makes 4 to 6 idlis.
Soaking time: 3 hours.   No fermenting.

½ cup toovar dal (arhar)
¼ cup split yellow gram (yellow moong dal)
½ cup split Bengal gram (chana dal)
1 cup chopped fenugreek (methi) leaves
2 cups chopped coriander
¼ cup green peas, boiled

¼ cup grated coconut
3 green chillies, chopped
1 small onion, chopped
1 small carrot, grated
salt to taste
oil for greasing

1. Wash and soak the dals together for at least 3 hours. Drain and grind to a smooth paste. Add the fenugreek leaves, coriander, green peas, coconut, green chillies, onion, carrot and salt.
2. Add water as required to make a thick batter.
3. Pour into greased idli moulds and steam for 10 to 12 minutes till done. Serve hot.

SAGO AND NACHNI DOSA : Recipe on page 47 ➙

⟡ QUICK RAWA IDLI ⟡

Soft semolina idlis that are quick to make. They require no fermenting.

Preparation time: 10 minutes.   Cooking time: 20 minutes.   Makes 14 to 16 idlis.
Soaking time: 30 minutes.   No fermenting.

2½ cups semolina (rawa)
4 cups buttermilk
1 tbsp fruit salt
2 tbsp oil
salt to taste
oil for greasing

For the tempering
1 tsp cumin seeds (jeera)
2 tbsp thinly sliced coconut
2 green chillies, chopped
4 curry leaves (kadi patta)
1 tbsp oil

1. Mix the semolina, buttermilk, oil and salt together in a bowl. Keep aside for 30 mins.
2. Prepare the tempering by heating the oil and adding the cumin seeds, coconut, green chillies and curry leaves. When the cumin seeds crackle, add the tempering to the semolina batter.
3. Add the fruit salt, mix well and pour the batter into greased idli moulds. Steam for 7 to 10 minutes. Serve hot with a chutney of your choice.

⤴ COOKED RICE IDLI ⤴

Velvety soft idlis made with cooked rice.

Preparation time: 20 minutes.   Cooking time: 30 minutes.   Makes 20 idlis.
Soaking time: 2 hours.   Fermenting time: Overnight.

½ cup split black gram (urad dal)
1 cup cooked rice
1 cup rice semolina (idli rawa)
salt to taste
oil for greasing

1. Wash and soak the urad dal for at least 2 hours in lukewarm water.
2. Grind it into a smooth batter along with the cooked rice.
3. Wash the idli rawa and add it to the batter along with the salt. (After adding the idli rawa, whip the mixture thoroughly so as to mix it well with the batter).
4. Mix well, cover and set aside overnight for fermenting.
5. Spoon out the batter into greased idli moulds and steam for 15 minutes.
   Serve hot with a chutney of your choice.

◎ SPINACH IDLI BAR ◎

This new version not only makes the humble idli look more colourful but also enhances its taste and nutrient value.

Preparation time: 30 minutes.   Cooking time: 30 minutes.   Makes 2 bars.

1 recipe poha idli batter, page 10
oil for greasing

For the spinach mixture
1 bunch spinach (palak), chopped
3 green chillies, chopped
1 onion, chopped
1 tbsp butter
1 tsp oil
salt to taste

For the spinach mixture
1. Heat the butter and oil in a pan.
2. Add the green chillies and onion and fry for some time.

3. Then add the spinach and salt and stir for some time.
4. Remove from the fire and keep aside.

How to proceed

1. Grease a non-stick rectangular mould 170 mm. x 120 mm. (6½" x 4½") and put a 5 mm. (⅕") thick layer of the spinach mixture on it.
2. Spoon out a 20 mm. (¾") layer of the idli batter on it
3. Steam for 10 minutes. Cool and unmould.
4. Repeat with the remaining batter to make 1 more bar.
   Serve hot with coconut sauce, page 92.

DOSAS

○ The dosa griddle is traditionally made of cast iron although non-stick tavas are more favoured now.

○ To prepare the tava / griddle, heat till it becomes very hot, sprinkle some water. It should evaporate quickly. Wipe with a soft cloth and reduce the flame. Then rub it with a thick slice of potato or onion dipped in oil. Your tava / griddle is now ready to use.

○ If your cast iron griddle is giving you trouble, pour half a cup of salt on it and heat on a medium flame for about 5 minutes while stirring continuously. Remove the salt and use.

○ The batter should always be at room temperature. So if you have refrigerated the batter, leave it at room temperature for about an hour before you proceed.

○ After spreading the dosa batter on the tava / griddle, pour a tsp of oil or ghee along the sides of the dosa in order to brown it evenly and to ensure that it does not stick to the tava / griddle.

๑ DOSA ๑

Picture on back cover.

The preparation which has put South India on every culinary hot spot of the world. Served traditionally with sambhar and chutney.

Preparation time: 20 minutes.   Cooking time: 20 minutes.   Makes 8 dosas.
Soaking time: 2 hours.   Fermenting time: 4 hours.

1 cup raw rice
1/3 cup split black gram (urad dal)
2 tbsp cooked rice
2 tbsp beaten rice (poha)
5 to 7 fenugreek (methi) seeds
salt to taste
oil for cooking

1. Wash the raw rice, urad dal and fenugreek seeds. Soak in a little water along with the beaten rice and cooked rice for at least 2 hours.
2. Grind to a smooth paste with a little water. Cover and keep aside for at least 4 hours. Add the salt and mix well.

3. Heat a non-stick tava and grease it lightly with oil. When hot, pour a ladleful of the batter, spread using a circular motion to make a thin dosa and cook on one side. Pour a little oil along the edges while cooking. When crispy, fold over and serve hot.
4. Repeat with the remaining batter to make more dosas.
   Serve with coconut chutney, page 73 and sambhar, page 84.

VARIATION: ## Masala Dosa

When the dosa is cooked, put some Potato Bhaji, page 82, on it. Roll to form a cylindrical shape and serve hot.

Corn and Paneer Dosa

When the dosa is cooked, put some Corn and Paneer Bhaji, page 83, on it. Roll to form a cylindrical shape and serve hot.

๑ TRICOLOUR UTTAPAM ๑

Uttapams with a difference.

Preparation time: 5 minutes.   Cooking time: 20 minutes.   Makes 8 to 10 uttapams.
Soaking time: 2 hours.   Fermenting time: 4 hours.

1 recipe dosa batter, page 25
3 small onions, chopped
2 tomatoes, chopped
¼ cup corn, boiled
¼ cup chopped capsicum
¼ cup grated carrot
3 tsp lemon juice
2 tbsp oil
salt to taste
oil for cooking

1. Heat the oil in a pan, add the onions and fry till they are golden brown.
2. Add the tomatoes and salt and stir for some time. Remove from the fire and keep aside.

3. Put the corn, capsicum and carrot in 3 small bowls.
4. Add 1 tsp of lemon juice and salt in each bowl. Mix well and keep aside.
5. Heat and grease a non-stick tava on a medium flame.
6. Put 1 ladle of the batter on it.
7. Spread 1 tbsp of the onion-tomato mixture on it.
8. Spread the corn, capsicum and carrots besides each other on top of this mixture so as to get three different coloured portions on your uttappam.
9. Cook till done on both the sides.
10. Repeat with the remaining batter and mixtures to make more uttapams.
    Serve hot with coconut chutney, page 73.

❧ NEER DOSA ❧

Soft and lacy rice pancakes.

Preparation time: 15 minutes.   Cooking time: 15 minutes.   Makes 12 to 15 dosas.
Soaking time: 2 hours.   No fermenting.

1 cup raw rice, soaked
salt to taste
oil for cooking

1. Soak the rice in water for at least 2 hours. Then drain and wash it.
2. Add water and grind to make a very fine batter.
3. Add salt and more water if necessary to make a thin batter of pouring consistency.
4. Heat a small non-stick tava and sprinkle a little water on it. It should steam immediately. Wipe hard with a slice of onion or potato.
5. Grease the tava with a little ghee and pour a ladleful of batter from a little height so that you get plenty of holes. Do not try to spread the batter with a spoon.
6. Cook the dosa on one side only taking care to see that it does not brown. Fold it twice to make a quarter circle.
7. Repeat with the remaining batter to make more dosas.
   Serve hot with Churna, page 79.

꧁ QUICK RICE DOSA ꧂

A dosa which you can rustle up whenever your guest drop in. A quicker version of the traditional Neer Dosa.

Preparation time: 5 minutes.   Cooking time: 20 minutes.   Makes 15 dosas.
No soaking.   No fermenting.

½ cup raw rice, washed
¼ cup grated coconut
¼ cup cooked rice
salt to taste
oil for cooking

1. Grind the raw rice, coconut and cooked rice along with ½ cup of water into a smooth batter.
2. Add the salt and adjust the consistency by adding water to make a thin watery batter.
3. Heat a small non-stick pan and sprinkle some water on it. It should be steaming immediately. Wipe hard with a slice of onion or potato.
4. Grease the pan lightly with oil.

5. Pour a ladleful of batter from a little height so that you get plenty of holes. Do not try to spread the batter with a spoon.
6. Fold it into half and then into a quarter to form a triangular shape.
7. Take care to see that the dosa does not become crisp as this is a soft dosa.
8. Repeat with the remaining batter to make more dosas.
   Serve hot with a chutney of your choice.

◎ MAIDA DOSA ◎

A quick and unusual soft dosa made of plain flour.

Preparation time: 10 minutes.   Cooking time: 20 minutes.   Makes 8 dosas.
No soaking.   No fermenting.

1¼ cup plain flour (maida)
½ cup grated coconut
1 tsp chopped green chillies
½ tsp sugar
salt to taste
oil for cooking

For the tempering
½ tsp mustard seeds (rai)
8 to 10 curry leaves (kadi patta)
1 tbsp oil

1. Grind the coconut, green chillies and sugar with a little water to make a smooth paste.
2. In a bowl, mix together the flour, coconut mixture, salt and ¾ cup of water and whisk well to make a smooth batter.
3. Prepare the tempering by heating the oil in a small bowl and adding the mustard seeds. When they crackle, add the curry leaves.
4. Pour this tempering over the batter and mix well.
5. Heat a non-stick tava on a medium flame till hot and grease it lightly with oil.
6. Pour a ladleful of the batter on the tava and spread it to get a dosa of 2 mm. thickness.
7. Smear a little oil from the sides and cook the dosa on a medium flame till evenly browned on one side.
8. Repeat with the remaining batter to make more dosas.
   Serve immediately.

VARIATION: **Moru Dosa**

Use thin buttermilk instead of coconut. Add the flour, green chilli paste, sugar and salt and mix well to make a smooth paste. Proceed as for Maida Dosa. Serve immediately.

◉ RAWA DOSA ◉

Crisp dosas made with a semolina and buttermik batter.

Preparation time: 30 minutes.   Cooking time: 12-15 minutes.   Makes 6 dosas.
No soaking.   Fermenting time: 15 to 20 minutes.

1 cup semolina (rawa)
2 tsp plain flour (maida)
½ cup curds
2 green chillies, chopped
½ tsp cumin seeds (jeera)
2 tbsp grated coconut
salt to taste
oil for cooking

1. Mix together the rawa, flour, curds and ½ cup of water to make a batter.
2. Cover and keep aside for 15 to 20 minutes.
3. Add the green chillies, cumin seeds, coconut and salt and mix well.
4. Add more water to make a thin batter.

34

5. Heat a large non-stick tava on a high flame and pour ½ cup of the batter while tilting the tava so that the batter forms a thin layer.
6. Smear a little oil on the sides.
7. When the sides brown evenly, fold over into half.
8. Repeat with the remaining batter to make more dosas.
   Serve hot.

VARIATION: **Rawa Uttapam**

You can make rawa uttapam with the same ingredients by using less water.

ଓ METHI GHAVAN ଓ

Picture on facing page.

A Maharashtrian version of the dosa.

Preparation time: 10 minutes.   Cooking time: 10 minutes.   Makes 4 ghavans.
No soaking.   No fermenting.

1 cup rice flour
2 green chillies, chopped
½ tsp grated ginger
¼ cup chopped fenugreek leaves (methi)
1 tsp cumin seeds (jeera)

½ tsp turmeric powder (haldi)
1 tsp oil
salt to taste
oil for cooking

1. Mix the rice flour in a bowl with enough water to get a pouring consistency batter.
2. Mix the rest of the ingredients in the batter and keep aside.
3. Heat a non-stick tava and grease it with oil. Pour 2 ladlefuls of the mixture on the tava and spread it evenly. Put a little oil on the sides.
4. Turn the ghavan upside down and cook till crisp and brown from both sides.
5. Repeat with the rest of the batter to make more ghavans. Serve hot.

METHI GHAVAN, Recipe above • RED GARLIC CHUTNEY : Recipe on page 77. ➜

◈ RICE RAWA DOSA ◈

Another version of rawa dosa.

Preparation time: 10 minutes.   Cooking time: 25 minutes.   Makes 12 dosas.
No soaking.   No fermenting.

1 cup semolina (rawa)
1 cup rice flour
a few cashewnut pieces
a few dried coconut pieces
¼ tsp soda bi-carb
salt to taste
ghee for cooking

For the tempering
½ tsp cumin seeds (jeera)
2 green chillies, chopped
a pinch asafoetida (hing)
a few curry leaves (kadi patta), chopped
3 tsp oil

1. Mix together the semolina, rice flour, soda bi-carb and salt and add enough water (approximately 4 cups) to make a very thin batter.
2. To prepare the tempering, heat the oil in a small vessel, add the cumin seeds and fry until they crackle. Add the green chillies, asafoetida and curry leaves and fry for a few seconds. Add this to the batter.
3. Add the cashewnut and coconut and mix well.
4. Heat a large non-stick pan on a high flame and grease it lightly with ghee. Pour ½ cup of the batter in circular manner.
5. Pour a little ghee in the holes of the dosa and cook until crisp.
6. Fold into a triangular shape and serve hot with Coconut Chutney, page 73, repeat with the remaining batter to make more dosas.

൭ PESARATTU ൭

Green gram dal dosas spiked with onion, green chillies and ginger.

Preparation time: 15 minutes.   Cooking time: 20 minutes.   Makes 6 to 8 pesarattus.
Soaking time: 4 hours.   No fermenting.

1 cup split green gram (green moong dal)
1 finely chopped onion
2 to 3 finely chopped green chillies
1 tsp grated ginger
salt to taste
oil for cooking

1. Wash and soak the split moong dal in water for at least 4 hours.
2. Drain and grind to a coarse paste.
3. Add the onion, green chillies, ginger and salt and mix well.
4. Heat a non-stick tava and grease it lightly with oil.

5. Spread a ladleful of the batter on the tava to make a 2 mm. thick dosa. Smear a little oil from the sides.
6. Cook on both sides till light brown.
7. Repeat with the remaining batter to make more peserattu. Serve hot.

VARIATION: **Pesarattu with Vegetable Stir-Fry**

Fill the pesarattu with a stir-fry of your choice and serve it with Coconut Sauce, page 92.

꩜ APPAM ꩜

Kerala is famous for appam. This recipe makes a difficult dish easy to cook.

Preparation time: 15 minutes.   Cooking time: 15 minutes.   Makes 10 to 15 appams.
Soaking time: 2 to 3 hours.   Fermenting time: 2 to 3 hours.

2 cups raw rice
½ cup cooked rice
1 coconut
2 tsp sugar
½ tsp dry yeast
salt to taste
oil for cooking

1. Wash and soak the rice for 2 to 3 hours. Drain.
2. Grate the coconut, add 2 cups of water and extract the coconut milk. Strain.
3. Grind the raw rice and cooked rice in a little coconut milk. Remove from the grinder and add the sugar, the remaining coconut milk and salt.
4. Mix the yeast with a little warm water, add to the rice paste and mix well. The

batter should be of dropping consistency.

5. Cover and keep for 2 to 3 hours.
6. Heat an appam kadai or a deep non-stick tava and grease it lightly with oil.
7. Pour 1 big spoon of the batter into it. Slowly rotate the batter on the tava so that a thin layer forms on the side while the middle remains thick.
8. Cover and cook for 1 minute. The middle part will be fluffy.
9. Repeat with the remaining batter to make more appams.
   Serve hot with Vegetable Stew, page 91.

VARIATION: Spinach Appam

Add 2 tbsp spinach purée to the batter at step 5.

☉ JAGGERY DOSA ☉

Soft pancake-like dosas that are flavoured with coconut, cardamom and jaggery.

Preparation time: 10 minutes.   Cooking time: 30 minutes.   Makes 10 to 12 dosas.
No soaking.   Fermenting time: 10 minutes.

½ cup rice flour
1 cup whole wheat flour (gehun ka atta)
½ cup grated jaggery (gur)

½ tsp cardamom (elaichi) powder
2 tbsp grated coconut
ghee for cooking

1. Combine all the ingredients in a bowl and add warm water to make a batter of dropping consistency. Allow to stand for 10 minutes and mix well.
2. Heat a non-stick tava and grease it lightly with ghee.
3. Pour one ladleful of the batter and spread it to make a circle of 2 mm. thickness.
4. Smear a little ghee on the top and turn over.
5. Cook till both sides are golden brown.
6. Repeat with the remaining batter to make more dosas.
   Serve hot.

☙ CORN DOSA ❧

For best results, use fresh sweet corncobs.

Preparation time: 10 minutes.   Cooking time: 10 to 20 minutes.   Serves 4.
No soaking.   No fermenting.

3 nos. sweet corncobs
9 tbsp Bengal gram flour (besan)
2 green chillies, chopped
4 tbsp chopped coriander
salt to taste
oil for cooking

1. Grate the sweet corn, add the gram flour, green chillies, coriander, salt and enough
   water to make a smooth batter of pouring consistency.
2. Heat a non-stick tava over a medium flame and grease it lightly with oil.
3. Pour a ladleful of the batter on the pan and swirl the pan so as to get a thin dosa.
4. Cook on both sides till golden brown.
5. Repeat with the remaining batter to make more dosas.
   Serve hot.

๑ **NACHNI DOSA** ๑

A wholesome dosa made with ragi.

Preparation time: 15 minutes.   Cooking time: 20 minutes.   Makes 6 dosas.
Soaking time: Overnight.   No fermenting.

1 cup ragi (nachni)
1 large onion, chopped
2 green chillies, chopped
1 tsp grated ginger
½ cup chopped coriander
salt to taste
oil for cooking

1. Soak the ragi in water overnight.
2. Drain and grind to a paste using a little water.
3. Add the chopped onion, green chillies, ginger, coriander and salt and mix well.
4. Heat a non-stick tava and grease it with a little oil.
5. Spread an even layer of the batter to make a 125 mm. (5") dosa.

6. Cook on both sides till golden brown, using a little oil.
7. Repeat with the rest of the batter to make more dosas.
   Serve hot.

VARIATION: Sago and Nachni Dosa (Picture on page 19.)

You can also add soaked sago seeds (sabudana) into the batter.

⊙ DAL AND RICE DOSA ⊙

Paper thin crisp dosas.

Preparation time: 20 minutes.   Cooking time: 30 minutes.   Makes 15 dosas.
Soaking time: 2 hours.   Fermenting time: Overnight.

1 cup raw rice
1 cup split black gram (urad dal)
1 cup split Bengal gram (chana dal)
salt to taste
oil for cooking

1. Wash and soak the rice, urad dal and chana dal in lukewarm water for at least 2
   hours. Drain, wash and grind to a smooth paste using ½ cup of water.
2. Cover and set aside to ferment overnight. Next day, add salt and enough water to
   make a thin batter.
3. Heat a non-stick tava on a medium flame till hot and grease it with oil.
4. Spread a ladleful of the batter on the pan to make a 200 mm. (8") diameter dosa.
5. Roast on one side till golden brown and crisp.
6. Repeat with the remaining batter to make more dosas.
   Serve hot with a chutney of your choice.

๑ CRISPY CUP DOSA ๑

This is called cup dosa because 1 cup of all ingredients are used to make it.

Preparation time: 15 minutes.   Cooking time: 20 minutes.   Makes 8 dosas.
Soaking time: 4 hours.   Fermenting time: Overnight.

1 cup split black gram (urad dal)
1 cup split Bengal gram (chana dal)
1 cup Bengal gram flour (besan)
salt to taste
oil for cooking

1. Soak the urad dal and chana dal in lukewarm water for at least 4 hours.
2. Wash, drain and grind to a smooth paste with a little water.
3. Cover and allow to ferment overnight.
4. Next day, add the gram flour, 1 cup of water and salt and mix well.
5. Heat a non-stick tava on a medium flame till hot and grease it with a little oil.
6. Spread one ladleful of the dasa batter thinly on the tava.

7. Pour some oil from the sides and roast the dosa on a medium flame till it is golden brown in colour.
8. Fold the dosa into half and remove from the tava.
9. Repeat with the remaining batter to make more dosas.
Serve hot with Malagapadi Powder, page 80.

๑ TOUSALI ๏

A sweet dosa made with tousa which is the local name for the big green cucumber used in this recipe.

Preparation time: 20 minutes. Cooking time: 20 minutes. Makes 8 tousalis.
Soaking time: 4 hours. Fermenting time: 4 hours.

1 cup raw rice
¾ cup grated coconut
½ cup grated jaggery (gur)
¾ cup grated cucumber
4 tbsp melted ghee
1 level tsp salt
oil for cooking

1. Soak the rice for at least 4 hours in lukewarm water.
2. Drain, wash and grind to a smooth paste along with the coconut, jaggery and ¼ cup of water.
3. Add the cucumber and salt and mix well.

4. If the batter is too thick, adjust the consistency by adding enough water to make a batter of dropping consistency.
5. Keep aside for 4 hours.
6. Heat a non-stick tava and grease it lightly with ghee.
7. Pour 1 ladleful of the batter on the hot tava and spread it to get a 3 to 4 mm. thick dosa.
8. Cover with a lid and cook only one side over a slow flame until the base is golden brown in colour and the top is firm.
9. Remove the tousali and repeat with the remaining batter to make more tousalis. Serve hot with ghee.

✍ SPICY TOUSALI ✍

Picture on page 55.

A *spicy version of the sweet tousali.*

Preparation time: 20 minutes.   Cooking time: 20 minutes.   Makes 8 tousalis.
Soaking time: 4 hours.   Fermenting time: 4 hours.

1 cup raw rice
½ cup grated coconut
¾ cup grated cucumber
2 tsp sugar
3 green chillies, chopped
4 to 5 tbsp curds
4 tbsp melted ghee
salt to taste
oil for cooking

1. Soak the rice for at least 4 hours in lukewarm water.
2. Drain, wash and grind to a smooth paste along with the coconut.
3. Add the cucumber, sugar, green chillies, curds and salt.

4. If the batter is too thick, adjust the consistency by adding enough water to make a batter of dropping consistency.
5. Keep aside for 4 hours.
6. Heat a non-stick tava and grease it lightly with ghee.
7. Pour 1 ladleful of the batter on the hot tava and spread it to get a 3 to 4 mm. thick dosa.
8. Cover with a lid and cook only one side over a slow flame until the base is golden brown in colour and the top is firm.
9. Remove the tousali and repeat with the remaining batter to make more tousalis. Serve hot with ghee or Churna, page 79.

SPICY TOUSALI : Recipe on page 53. ➜

⌕ MOONG DAL DOSA ⌕

Thin, crisp dosas made of moong dal and rice.

Preparation time: 10 minutes.   Cooking time: 25 minutes.   Makes 10 to 12 dosas.
Soaking time: 3 hours.   Fermenting time: 8 hours.

1 cup split green gram (green moong dal)
1 cup parboiled rice
salt to taste
oil for cooking

1. Wash and soak the moong dal and rice in water for at least 3 hours.
2. Grind to a fine paste using a little water.
3. Cover and allow to ferment for at least 8 hours.
4. Adjust the consistency of the batter by adding water if required. The batter should
   be of dropping consistency.

5. Heat and grease a non-stick tava with oil.
6. Pour a ladleful of the batter on the tava and spread it using a circular motion.
7. Pour a little oil on the sides and cook.
8. When the lower side is golden brown, fold over.
9. Repeat with the remaining batter to make more dosas.
   Serve immediately with chutney.

❀ PAPER DOSA ❀

A thin crisp dosa.

Preparation time: 10 minutes.   Cooking time: 15 minutes.   Makes 10 to 12 dosas.
Soaking time: 4 hours.   Fermenting time: 10 to 12 hours.

½ cup raw rice
¾ cup split black gram (urad dal)
½ cup rice flour
salt to taste
oil for cooking

1. Wash and soak the raw rice and urad dal for about 4 hr. Drain, mix the rice flour and grind to a smooth paste using enough water to get a batter of coating consistency.
2. Heat a non-stick tava and grease it lightly with oil. When hot, pour a ladleful of the batter and spread it using circular motion to make a paper thin dosa. Cook on one side, pouring a little oil along the edges while cooking. When crisp, make a roll and serve hot.
3. Repeat with the remaining batter to make more dosas.
   Serve hot with coconut chutney, page 73, and Sambhar, page 84.

❀ SET DOSA ❀

Picture on page 2.

An amazing soft dosa.

Preparation time: 10 minutes.   Cooking time: 25 minutes.   Makes 10 to 12 dosas.
Soaking time: 4 hours.   Fermenting time: Overnight (10 to 12 hours).

½ cup parboiled rice
½ cup raw rice
¼ cup split black gram (urad dal)
a pinch baking soda
salt to taste
oil for cooking

1. Wash and soak the parboiled rice, raw rice and urad dal together for 4 hours.
2. Drain and grind to a smooth paste adding enough water to make a batter of dropping consistency.
3. Cover and keep aside to ferment for 10 to 12 hours.
4. Then add the baking soda and salt and mix well.

5. Grease and heat a small non-stick pan on medium flame and pour a ladleful of the batter on it.
6. Spread the batter to get a 5 mm. thick dosa.
7. Cover and cook till one side is golden brown.
   Repeat with the remaining batter to make more dosas.
   Serve hot with a chutney of your choice.

SOYA GOODIES

Soyabeans are an ideal source of protein and have been found to have rejuvenating properties. They also provide the nutrition essential for the maintenance of health and resistance to various diseases.

So, even if the dishes are a little time consuming to make, the health benefits surely make it worth all the efforts you put in.

∽ SOYA MILK ∽

Soaked soyabean extract.

Preparation time: a few minutes.   No cooking.   Makes about 500 ml.
Soaking time: 3 hours.   No fermenting.

1 cup soyabeans

1. Wash and soak the soyabeans in water for at least 3 hours.
2. Drain out all the water.
3. Blend in a mixer with 3 cups of water to a fine purée.
4. Strain through a fine strainer to extract the milk.

Handy tip : Do not keep this milk for very long as it emits an odour after an hour or
so. Best if used immediately.

๑ SOYA DOSA ๑

High protein wheat flour and soya pancakes.

Preparation time: 2 minutes.   Cooking time: 15 minutes.   Makes 6 dosas.
No soaking.   No fermenting.

1 cup soya milk, page 62
¼ cup whole wheat flour (gehun ka atta)
1 green chilli, chopped
1 onion, grated

1 tbsp chopped coriander
¼ tsp fruit salt
salt to taste
oil for cooking

1. Make a thin batter using the soya milk, wheat flour, green chilli, onion, coriander, fruit salt, salt and water. Mix well.
2. Heat a non-stick tava and grease it with oil.
3. Pour 2 tbsp of the batter on the tava and spread it using a circular motion.
4. Cook on both sides using a little oil.
5. Repeat with the remaining batter to make more dosas.
   Serve hot.

꧁ INSTANT SOYA UTTAPAM ꧂

Picture on facing page.

Delicious protein-rich uttapam.

Preparation time: 10 minutes. Cooking time: 20 minutes. Makes 6 uttapams.
No soaking. Fermenting time: 10 minutes.

2 cups thick soya milk, page 62
1 cup semolina (rawa)
2 green chillies, chopped
1 tomato, chopped
1 onion, chopped

2 tbsp chopped coriander
½ tsp fruit salt
salt to taste
oil for cooking

1. Combine the soya milk and semolina in a bowl and keep aside for 10 minutes.
2. Add the green chillies, tomato, onion, coriander, fruit salt and salt and mix well.
3. Heat a non-stick tava and grease it with oil.
4. Pour a ladleful of the batter and spread it using a circular motion.
5. Cook on both sides using oil.
6. Repeat with the remaining batter to make more dosas.
   Serve hot.

INSTANT SOYA UTTAPAM : Recipe above. ➜

APPES

Dumplings of fermented batter of rice and dals steamed in the traditional appe moulds.

◎ PULSE APPE ◎

Appes are cooked in special appe moulds.

Preparation time: 20 minutes.   Cooking time: 40 minutes.   Makes about 25 appes.
Soaking time: 2 hours.   Fermenting time: Overnight.

¾ cup split Bengal gram (chana dal)
¼ cup toovar dal (arhar)
1 tbsp split green gram (moong dal)
1 tsp split black gram (urad dal)
½ cup parboiled rice
½ cup raw rice
1 cup chopped spinach (palak)

salt to taste
oil for cooking

For the tempering
1 onion, chopped
½ tsp chilli powder
4 to 5 curry leaves (kadi patta)
a pinch turmeric powder (haldi)
a pinch asafoetida (hing)
3 tbsp oil

1. Soak the chana dal, toovar dal, moong dal, urad dal, parboiled rice and raw rice in lukewarm water for at least for 2 hours.
2. Grind to a smooth paste with a little water.
3. Cover and keep aside overnight.
4. Next day, add enough water to get a batter of dropping consistency.
5. Add the spinach and salt.
6. Make a tempering by heating the oil and adding the onion, chilli power, curry leaves, turmeric powder and asafoetida and heating it till the onion turns light brown.
7. Add this tempering to the batter and mix well.

8. Heat the appe mould on a medium flame and grease it with a little oil.
9. Pour a spoonful of the batter into each mould.
10. Cook till the outer surface becomes golden brown and then turn each appe upside down using a fork so as to cook the other side.
11. Remove and repeat with the remaining batter to make more appes.
    Serve hot with Coconut Chutney, page 73.

VARIATION: You may add boiled corn instead of spinach.

◎ SEMOLINA APPE ◎

Appes made of semolina and curds.

Preparation time: 10 minutes.   Cooking time: 40 minutes.   Makes 25 appes.
No soaking.   Fermenting time: 4 hours.

1½ cups semolina (rawa)
1 cup curds
2 tomatoes, chopped
2 onions, chopped
2 green chillies, chopped
salt to taste

1. Beat the curds with ½ cup of water and then add the semolina and salt to make batter of dropping consistency.
2. Cover and keep aside for 4 hours to ferment.
3. Then, add the tomatoes, onions and green chillies to the fermented batter.
4. Heat the appe mould on a medium flame and grease it with a little oil.
5. Pour a spoonful of the batter into each mould.

6. Cook till the outer surface becomes golden brown and then turn each appe upside down using a fork so as to cook the other side.
7. Remove and repeat with the remaining batter.
   Serve hot with coconut chutney, page 73.

๑ RICE APPE ๑

Picture on page 75.

Traditional appes made with rice.

Preparation time: 20 minutes.   Cooking time: 40 minutes.   Makes 20 to 24 appes.
Soaking time: 2 hours.   Fermenting time: Overnight.

1 cup raw rice
¼ cup split black gram (urad dal)
¼ cup crushed peanuts
2 tbsp chopped onions
1 tsp mustard seeds (rai)
1 tsp cumin seeds (jeera)
2 green chillies, chopped
8 to 10 curry leaves (kadi patta)
a pinch asafoetida (hing)
2 tbsp oil
salt to taste
oil for cooking

1. Wash and soak the rice and urad dal in lukewarm water for at least 2 hours.
2. Drain and grind to a smooth paste with ½ cup of water.
3. Cover and set aside overnight to ferment.
4. Next day, heat the oil in a small kadhai, add the crushed peanuts and chopped onions and stir for 3 to 5 minutes. Add the mustard seeds, cumin seeds, green chillies, curry leaves and asafoetida. When the mustard and cumin seeds crackle, add this to the fermented batter.
5. Add salt and a little water if required and mix to form a thick batter.
6. Heat the appe mould on a medium flame and grease it with a little oil.
7. Pour a spoonful of the batter into each mould.
8. Cook till the outer surface becomes golden brown and then turn each appe upside down using a fork so as to cook the other side.
9. Remove and repeat with the remaining batter to make more appes.
   Serve hot with Tomato Chutney, page 74.

ACCOMPANIMENTS

COCONUT CHUTNEY

Picture on cover.

Preparation time: 10 minutes.   Cooking time: 15 minutes.   Makes 1 cup.

1 cup grated coconut
2 small green chillies, chopped
1 tsp grated ginger
1 tbsp roasted split gram (daria dal), optional
salt to taste

For the tempering
½ tsp mustard seeds (rai)
1 red chilli, broken into pieces
2 to 3 curry leaves (kadi patta)
1 tsp oil

1. Put the coconut, green chillies, ginger, roasted split gram and salt in a blender with a little water and grind to make a fine paste. Keep aside.
2. Prepare the tempering by heating the oil and adding the mustard seeds, red chilli and curry leaves and stirring till mustard seeds crackle. Pour this tempering over the chutney and mix well. Refrigerate and use as required.

๑ TOMATO CHUTNEY ๑

Picture on facing page.

Preparation time: 10 minutes.   Cooking time: 15 minutes.   Makes 1 cup.

2 tbsp split Bengal gram (chana dal)
1 onion, chopped
3 to 4 curry leaves (kadi patta)
2 red chillies
¼ tsp turmeric powder (haldi)
¼ tsp asafoetida (hing)
1 cup chopped tomatoes
1 tbsp oil
salt to taste

For the tempering
½ tsp mustard seeds (rai)
2 red chillies
1 tbsp oil

1. Wash the dal and keep aside.
2. Heat the oil in a pan, add the washed dal and stir till it becomes golden brown in colour.
3. Add the onion, curry leaves, red chillies, turmeric powder and asafoetida and fry

RICE APPE : Recipe on page 71 • TOMATO CHUTNEY : Recipe above. ↪

for a few minutes.

4. Then add the chopped tomatoes and fry for about 5 minutes to soften them.
5. Remove from the fire and cool to room temperature.
6. Put the tomato mixture in a blender, add salt and a little water and grind to a coarse paste.
7. Prepare the tempering by heating the oil in a small bowl and adding the mustard seeds and red chillies and frying till the seeds crackle.
8. Pour the tempering over the chutney and mix well.
9. Refrigerate and use as required.

◌ **CORIANDER-ONION CHUTNEY** ◌

Preparation time: 10 minutes.   Cooking time: 10 minutes.   Makes 1 cup.

¼ cup split black gram (urad dal)
1 cup chopped onions
¼ tsp asafoetida (hing)
1 tbsp tamarind pulp (imli)
2 red chillies

¼ cup chopped coriander
2 tbsp oil
salt to taste

For the tempering
½ tsp mustard seeds (rai)
2 red chillies, broken into pieces
1 tsp oil

1. Wash and soak the dal for 15 minutes.
2. Heat the oil in a pan, add the soaked dal and fry till it browns lightly.
3. Add the onion, asafoetida, tamarind pulp, red chillies and salt and fry for a few minutes. Cool and keep aside.
4. Put the dal and onion mixture and the coriander into a blender. Add ¼ cup of water and grind to a coarse paste.
5. Prepare the tempering by heating the oil in a pan, adding the mustard seeds and frying till they crackle. Add the red chillies and fry for a few seconds and then pour the tempering over the chutney. Mix well.
6. Refrigerate and use as required.

❍ RED GARLIC CHUTNEY ❍

Picture on page 37.

Preparation time: 10 minutes.   Cooking time: a few minutes.   Makes 1 cup.

1 cup grated coconut
6 to 7 cloves garlic, crushed
3 small red chillies

1 tsp tamarind pulp (imli)
1 tsp oil
salt to taste

1. Heat the oil in a saucepan and sauté the garlic and red chillies for ½ minute.
2. Add the coconut and stir for 1 more minute.
3. Cool and grind to a coarse paste with the tamarind and salt using a little water.
4. Refrigerate till ready to serve.

◌ MYSORE CHUTNEY ◌

Preparation time: a few minutes. Cooking time: 5 minutes. Makes ¾ cup.

½ cup split Bengal gram (chana dal)
1 tbsp split black gram (urad dal)
2 to 3 red chillies
½ tbsp tamarind pulp (imli)
½ tsp peppercorns

2 tsp grated jaggery (gur)
¾ cup grated coconut
2 tbsp oil
salt to taste

1. Heat the oil in a pan and roast the chana dal and urad dal till they become golden brown.
2. Add the red chillies and fry for 2 minutes.
3. Add the tamarind, peppercorns, jaggery and coconut and fry for a while. Cool for some time.
4. When cool, grind with salt to a smooth paste, adding a little water if needed.
5. This chutney is used to make Mysore Dosa. A thin layer is spread on the inside of the dosa.

๑ CHURNA ๏

Preparation time: 5 minutes. Cooking time: 1 minutes. Makes 1 cup.

¾ cup grated coconut
¼ cup grated jaggery (gur)
1 tsp green cardamom (elaichi) powder

1. Melt the jaggery in a saucepan.
2. Add the grated coconut and green cardamom and mix well.
3. Cool and keep aside.
   Serve with Neer Dosa, page 29, or Quick Rice Dosa, page 30.

MALAGAPADI POWDER

Preparation time: 5 minutes. Cooking time: 20 minutes. Makes 1 cup.

2 tbsp coriander (dhania) seeds
1½ tbsp cumin seeds (jeera)
2 tbsp split Bengal gram (chana dal)
2 tbsp split black gram (urad dal)
2 tbsp sesame seeds (till)
12 red chillies
1 tsp asafoetida (hing)
salt to taste

1. Mix and roast all the ingredients.
2. When roasted, powder and store in an air-tight container.

☙ CURRY LEAVES CHUTNEY POWDER ☙

Preparation time: 10 minutes.   Cooking time: 15 minutes.   Makes 1 cup.

½ cup grated dry coconut
¼ cup roasted split gram (daria dal)
25 curry leaves (kadi patta)
2 red chillies
1 tsp sesame seeds (til)
½ tsp tamarind pulp
salt to taste

1. Dry roast the coconut, split gram, curry leaves, red chillies and sesame seeds separately till crisp.
2. Combine together and grind the fine powder along with the tamarind pulp and salt.
   Serve with idlis or dosas.

Note: Roasted split gram is the roasted chana dal which is put in chaats.

⊙ POTATO BHAJI ⊚

Picture on back cover.

Preparation time: 10 minutes.   Cooking time: 15 minutes.   Makes 2 cups.

3 large potatoes, peeled and boiled
1 tsp mustard seeds (rai)
5 to 6 curry leaves (kadi patta)
4 green chillies, chopped
5 small onions, chopped
a pinch turmeric powder (haldi)

2 tbsp grated coconut
juice of 1 lemon
¼ cup chopped coriander
2 tbsp oil
salt to taste

1. Mash the potatoes and keep aside.
2. Heat the oil in a pan and add the mustard seeds to it.
3. When they crackle, add the curry leaves, green chillies and onions and stir till the onions turn golden brown.
4. Add the mashed potatoes, turmeric powder, coconut, lemon juice, coriander and salt and mix well.
5. Remove from the heat and keep aside.
   Use as required.

CORN AND PANEER BHAJI

Preparation time: 10 minutes.   Cooking time: 10 minutes.   Makes 2 cups.

1 cup sweet corn kernels
1 cup cubed paneer
1 onion, chopped
2 green chillies, finely chopped
¼ tsp turmeric powder (haldi)
½ tsp sugar
2 tbsp chopped coriander
2 tbsp oil
salt to taste

1. Heat the oil in a pan and sauté the onion and green chillies.
2. Add the sweet corn kernels, paneer, turmeric, sugar and some water.
3. Heat till the sweet corn kernels get cooked and then add the coriander.
4. Remove from the heat and keep aside.
   Serve with dosas.

⌾ SAMBHAR ⌾

Preparation time: 20 minutes.   Cooking time: 15 minutes.   Serves 4 to 6.

For the sambhar
1 cup toovar dal (arhar)
1 tomato, chopped
1 onion, chopped
2 brinjals, cubed
1 drumstick, cut into 4 pieces
1 potato, peeled and cubed
1 tbsp tamarind pulp (imli)
salt to taste

For the tempering
1 tsp mustard seeds (rai)
6 curry leaves (kadi patta)
¼ tsp asafoetida (hing)
2 tbsp oil

For the sambhar masala
6 to 8 red chillies
1 tbsp coriander (dhania) seeds
1 tsp fenugreek (methi) seeds
1 tbsp toovar dal (arhar)
1 tbsp split Bengal gram (chana dal)
1 tbsp split black gram (urad dal)
1 tsp turmeric powder (haldi)
½ tsp asafoetida (hing)
1 tsp oil

SPICY TAVA IDLIS : Recipe on page 93. ➜

For the sambhar masala
1. Heat the oil and roast all the ingredients for the sambhar masala in it
2. Grind to a fine paste in a blender using a little water. Keep aside.

How to proceed
1. Wash and pressure cook the dal, tomato, onion, brinjals, drumstick and potato with 2 cups of water.
2. Then add the tamarind pulp, sambhar masala, salt and 4 cups of water and bring to boil.
3. Prepare the tempering by heating the oil and frying the mustard seeds, curry leaves and asafoetida until the mustard seeds crackle. Add this to the sambhar and simmer for 15 minutes.
   Serve hot.

๏ KOLUMBU ๏

Preparation time: 20 minutes.   Cooking time: 45 minutes.   Serves 8.

For the kolumbu powder
1½ tbsp spit Bengal gram (chana dal)
1½ tbsp split black gram (urad dal)
1½ tbsp coriander (dhania) seeds
¼ tsp fenugreek (methi) seeds
½ tsp cumin seeds (jeera)
¼ tsp mustard seeds (rai)
5 peppercorns
½ tsp asafoetida (hing)
4 red chillies
¼ tsp turmeric powder (haldi)

For the kolumbu
1 cup toovar dal (arhar), cooked
1 cup cauliflower florets
½ cup french beans, strung and cut
1 cup potato cubes

1 cup brinjal cubes
2 cups drumstics
salt to taste

For the tempering
1 tsp mustard seeds (rai)
1 tsp asafoetida (hing)
7 to 8 curry leaves (kadi patta)
2 tbsp oil

For the kolumbu powder
1. Dry roast all the ingredients together.
2. Grind to a fine powder.

For the kolumbu
1. Cook the toovar dal with salt and water.
2. When half done, add the kolumbu powder, all the vegetables and salt and heat till they are cooked.
3. Prepare the tempering by heating the oil, adding the mustard seeds, asafoetida and curry leaves and frying for some time. When the seeds crackle, add this tempering to the kolumbu.
   Serve hot.

❧ CORN SAMBHAR ❧

Preparation time: 20 minutes.   Cooking time: 15 minutes.   Serves 8.

4 nos. grated corncobs
1 cup potatoes, cubed
1 cup Madras onions, peeled
½ recipe sambhar masala, page 84.
salt to taste

For the tempering
1 tsp mustard seeds (rai)
10 curry leaves (kadi patta)
a pinch asafoetida (hing)
2 tbsp oil

For the garnish
2 tbsp chopped coriander

1. Prepare the tempering by heating the oil in a large pan, adding the mustard seeds and frying until they crackle. Add the curry leaves and asafoetida.
2. Add the potatoes, Madras onions and 3 cups of water and sauté for a few minutes.
3. Add the sambhar masala and sauté for 2 minutes.
4. Add the corn and salt and simmer with 3 cups of water till the potatoes are soft. Serve hot garnished with the coriander.

๑ VEGETABLE STEW ๑

Picture on page 2.

Preparation time: 15 minutes.   Cooking time: 10 minutes.   Makes 3 cups.

1 coconut
2 cups mixed boiled vegetables (carrots, potatoes, french beans, cauliflower)
1 onion, chopped
2 cardamoms (elaichi)
2 cloves (laung)
2 small sticks cinnamon (dalchini)
2 chopped green chillies
1 tsp cornflour
1 tbsp oil
salt to taste

1. Grate the coconut, add 2 cups of water and take out coconut milk. Strain, add the cornflour and mix well (You can also use 2 cups of ready coconut milk instead).
2. Heat the oil in a tava and fry the onion for 1 minute. Add the cardamoms, cloves and cinnamon and fry again add the green chillies and salt and fry again.
3. Add the coconut milk and vegetables and cook for a few minutes. Remove from the fire. Serve hot.

๑ COCONUT SAUCE ๑

Preparation time: 5 minutes.   Cooking time: 5 minutes.   Makes 1 cup.

1 cup coconut milk
2 tsp cornflour
½ tsp cumin seeds (jeera)
2 curry leaves (kadi patta)
2 tsp green chilli paste
1 tsp lemon juice
½ tsp sugar
1 tbsp oil
salt to taste

1. Heat the oil in a saucepan.
2. Add the cumin seeds, curry leaves and green chilli paste and stir for 1 minute.
3. Add the coconut milk and cornflour and bring to a boil.
4. Add the lemon juice, sugar and salt and mix well.
5. Remove from the fire and serve hot.

LEFT-OVERS

◎ SPICY TAVA IDLIS ◎

Picture on page 85.

A spicy recipe guaranteed to polish off left-over idlis inspired by the famous pav-bhaji.

Preparation time: 15 minutes.   Cooking time: 15 minutes.   Serves 4.

4 leftover idlis, cut into cubes
1 onion, chopped
2 tomatoes, chopped
1 tsp grated ginger
1 tsp turmeric powder (haldi)
½ tsp black salt (snachal)
¼ tsp pav bhaji masala
1 tsp lemon juice
1 tbsp butter

1 tbsp oil
salt to taste

For the garnish
2 tbsp chopped coriander

1. Heat the oil and butter together, add the onions and fry till they soften.
2. Add the tomatoes, ginger and turmeric powder and cook till the oil separates.
3. Add the black salt, pav bhaji masala, salt and lemon juice and mix together.
4. Toss in the idlis and mix well.
   Serve hot garnished with the chopped coriander.

෧ IDLI UPMA ෨

A *very tasty snack of left-over idlis.*

Preparation time: 5 minutes.   Cooking time: 5 minutes.   Serves 2.

6 leftover idlis
1 tsp mustard seeds (rai)
2 red chillies, broken into pieces
½ carrot, chopped

¼ cup green peas, boiled
1 tomato, chopped
2 tbsp oil
salt to taste

1. Crumble all the idlis. Keep aside.
2. Heat the oil in a pan, add the red chillies and mustard seeds and fry for some time. When the mustard seeds crackle, add the carrot, peas and ¼ cup of water.
3. Cover and cook till the vegetables are tender.
4. Add the tomatoes and fry for some time.
5. Add the crumbled idlis and mix lightly so as not to mash the idlis. Serve hot.

⑥ DOSA LASAGNE ⑥

An Innovative way of using left-over dosas and masala bhaji.

Preparation time: 10 minutes.   Cooking time: 10 minutes.   Serves 2.
Baking time: 15 minutes.   Baking temperature: 180°C (350°F).

2 leftover dosas
1 cup potato bhaji, page 82
1 recipe coconut sauce, page 92
salt to taste
oil for greasing

1. Grease a rectangular tin of 170 mm. x 120 mm. x 60 mm. (6½" x 4½" x 2¼").
2. Cut the dosas into thick strips and soak them in the coconut sauce.
3. Put one dosa at the base of the tin.
4. Spread half the potato bhaji on it and top with a ladleful of the coconut sauce.
5. Repeat steps 3, 4 and 5.
6. Bake in a pre-heated oven at 180°C (350°F) for 10 to 12 minutes.
7. Cool slightly, unmould and cut into slices.
   Serve hot.

⊙ IDLI CURRY ⊚

A *sweet and tangy curry.*

Preparation time: 5 minutes.   Cooking time: 20 minutes.   Serves 4.

8 leftover idlis, cut into pieces
2 onions, chopped
½ tsp ginger paste
½ cup tomato purée
½ cup green peas
1 tsp sambhar masala, page 84
½ tsp chilli powder
a pinch sugar
¼ cup milk
3 tbsp oil
salt to taste

For the garnish
2 tbsp chopped coriander

1. Heat 2 tbsp of oil in shallow frying pan. Fry the idli pieces till golden brown and keep aside.
2. Heat the remaining oil in the same pan. Add the onions and ginger paste and fry for some time.
3. Add the tomato pureé, green peas, sambhar masala, chilli powder, sugar and salt the heat till the peas are cooked.
4. Then add 1 cup of water and ¼ cup of milk and boil the curry. Keep aside.
5. When you are ready to serve, heat the curry and add the idli pieces.
   Serve hot garnished with the coriander.

๑ SOUTH INDIAN SIZZLER ๑

A *sizzler made of idlis and dosas.*

Preparation time: 15 minutes.   Cooking time: 15 minutes.   Make 1 sizzler.

2 leftover idlis, cut into strips
1 masala dosa, page 26
½ cup Madras onions, peeled
½ green capsicum, sliced
½ yellow capsicum, sliced
½ red capsicum, sliced
1 spring onion, sliced
2 tsp lemon juice
2 tbsp butter
salt and pepper to taste

For the garnish
1 sprig parsley

1. Heat 1 tbsp of butter in a pan. Add the idli strips and sauté for some time. Transfer them onto a plate and keep aside.
2. In the same pan, add ½ tbsp of butter and sauté the Madras onions till they are translucent. Add salt and mix well. Keep aside.
3. Heat a sizzler plate and melt ½ tbsp of butter on it.
4. Add the capsicum and spring onion and stir-fry for some time.
5. Then add the Madras onions, idli strips, lemon juice, salt and pepper and mix well.
6. Cut the masala dosa into two and place each part on either side of the sizzler plate. Serve hot garnished with a sprig of parsley.

⌒ DOSA ENCHILADAS ⌒

When served this way the leftover dosa tastes nicer than the fresh one.

Preparation time: 15 minutes.   Cooking time: 30 minutes.   Serves 4.
Baking time: 10 minutes.   Baking temperature: 250°C (500°F).

2 left-over dosas, cut into pieces
¼ cup grated cooking cheese

For the stuffing
½ can (450 grams for full can) baked beans
1 large onion, finely chopped
4 cloves finely chopped garlic
1 tsp chilli powder
2 tbsp grated cheese
a pinch dried oregano
1 tbsp butter

For the sauce
3 large red tomatoes, sliced
½ onion, chopped
2 cloves finely chopped garlic
1 tbsp tomato ketchup
3 tbsp tomato pureé
2 tbsp sugar (approxi.)
1 tsp chilli powder
4 tbsp cream
1 tbsp oil
salt to taste

For the stuffing
1. Heat the butter in a pan, add the onion and garlic to it and sauté for 2 minutes.
2. Add the baked beans and chilli powder and cook further for 2 more minutes.
3. Remove from fire and add the cheese and oregano.
   Keep aside.

For the sauce
1. Pressure cook the tomatoes and onion with 2 tbsp of water upto 1 whistle.
2. Put in a blender and make a smooth paste.
3. Heat the oil in a large saucepan, add the garlic, the prepared paste, tomato ketchup, tomato pureé, sugar, chilli powder and salt and cook for a few minutes.
4. Add the cream and give one boil. Keep aside.

For the Enchiladas
1. Put 1 tbsp of the stuffing on one dosa piece and make a roll.
2. Repeat for all the pieces and stuffing.
3. Place the rolls on a baking dish and pour the hot sauce on them.
4. Sprinkle with the cheese and bake in a pre-heated oven at 250°C (500°F) until the cheese melts.
   Serve hot.

Mini Series by *Tarla Dalal*

7 Dinner Menus

Forever Young Diet

Nutritious Recipes for Pregnancy

Healthy Subzis

High Blood Pressure Cookbook

Low Calorie Sweets

Good Food for Diabetes

Healthy Snacks for Kids

Iron Rich Recipes

Low Cholesterol Recipes

Healthy Juices

Healthy Breakfast

Healthy Snacks

Healthy Soups & Salads

Calcium Rich Recipes

Home Remedies

Fast Foods made Healthy